A GUNDOG HANDLER'S
GUIDE TO
PICKING UP

A GUNDOG HANDLER'S GUIDE TO
PICKING UP

Veronica Heath

SWAN·HILL
PRESS

First published in the UK in 1999
by Swan Hill Press, an imprint of Airlife Publishing Ltd

British Library Cataloguing-in-Publication Data
  A catalogue record for this book
  is available from the British Library

ISBN 1 84037 007 6

Typeset by Rowland Phototypesetting Ltd, Bury St Edmunds, Suffolk.
Printed in England by St Edmundsbury Press Ltd, Bury St Edmunds,
Suffolk.

Swan Hill Press

an imprint of Airlife Publishing Ltd
101 Longden Road, Shrewsbury, SY3 9EB, England

Contents

Chapter 1

<u>What is Picking Up?</u>

Harvesting dead and wounded game shot by the guns on shoots is an important part of every shoot's economics. Every shoot, however small, needs pickers up. These are gundog handlers who may be professional dog trainers or amateurs, and the work has become so popular that it is now almost a field sport in its own right. It is a satisfying occupation, provides a humane service to the shoots concerned, keeps you fit and enables you to meet all kinds of interesting people. Although every shoot, however small, needs pickers up, the number of dogs and, therefore, people to handle them, does vary

On large pheasant shoots several men with gundogs are employed to collect the slain birds. Pickers up are seen here on a driven pheasant day in Northumberland.

according to the type of shooting and the number of guns out on a particular day. There are three likely scenarios for the work: on a grouse moor, on a pheasant or partridge shoot and, to a lesser extent, on a walked-up or rough shoot. Wildfowlers need their birds collected too but I think the guns invariably take their own retrievers because it is a solitary type of shooting entailing a lot of waiting about at unseasonal hours and I would not classify work in this context as the sort of retrieving that my readers will easily have access to.

When I started picking up thirty-five years ago, amateurs were very much in the minority. Almost without exception, pickers up were gamekeepers of which there were far more than there are today. I remember veteran beaters helping out too but there were almost no women. Those of us who did show interest were often regarded with suspicion, on a few occasions I was made to feel I was stepping out of line. I should have been beside my husband at his peg. In fact I retreated to the beating line where I made many friends, watched what was going on and generally got a foot in the door. Today the situation is different. Thousands of amateur gundog handlers, as well as professional gundog trainers now work as pickers up on shoots the length of Britain and women are welcomed. This has come about partly because the need for people with good retrievers has escalated and also because amateur handlers have become very good at the work. During the last fifteen years commercial shoots have multiplied which means more pheasant birds are put down and therefore more slain. Travelling syndicates are popular, this means a group of guns who have clubbed together to take a day, or a series of days, shooting on an estate. Many of these guns are, inevitably, not accompanied by dogs so this has meant more work for the picker up. Especially on the grouse moor, foreign guns are sometimes in the butts and they will certainly have no dogs accompanying them. Every effort must be made to gather wounded birds because everyone provides revenue for the shoot concerned. If a picker up gathers four or five cripples which are priced at £15 to £18 each (bought pheasants for the day) that is nearly £100 saved for the shoot and denied the fox. Where grouse are concerned, you can triple that sum.

What is it about the work that has attracted so many people to give it a try? Well primarily it must be the satisfaction of working a good dog. There is nothing to compare with that magic moment when your young canine trainee returns after a long and difficult retrieve with the lost bird in his mouth. And I like being part of a team committed to showing sport of a high order. There is also the closeness to nature; I've seen more wildlife picking up than at any other time, apart from roe stalking. It is the sun, the wind, the rain, the frost which make it so worthwhile, even when the elements are as unkind as the work is demanding, it is immensely rewarding. There have been days when I have had to stand under dripping branches in the teeth of a north-easterly straight off the sea for what seems like hours between drives, or when my dogs have had an off day and behaved like morons but I can honestly say that I have almost always enjoyed myself. By the time you have read this book you will know that it is not a job suited to couch potatoes.

Who is likely to want to get onto a picking up team? A broad spectrum of characters in my experience. I have had letters enquiring about the work and how to get started from company chairmen, retired army personnel, engineers and secretaries, to say nothing of housewives. Several guns I know who are not crack shots, have found that the challenges of handling their dog and harvesting the game are more satisfying than the art of shooting it. They have become pickers up and very good some of them are too because they know what it is like to stand at a peg, as well as a hundred yards behind it. Working tests are popular and some amateur handlers want to move on to working with live game, rather than progressing to field trials. Wives accompanying husbands or partners sometimes find standing and praising their man's skill at the peg or in a butt tedious. They want to get involved.

That is how I started. My husband had a gun in a small pheasant syndicate and in a grouse moor. I did spend a couple of years beside him, then my father gave him a small Labrador. The dog had all the right credentials but having retrieved a bird she refused to bring it in. The dog loved her master, they had bonded well and enjoyed one another's company and I was anxious not to interfere. And in those days I was too ignorant to know how to do so anyway. But I thought I could make myself useful on his shoots if I had a dog of my own. So I remained dogless for another season and joined the beaters to study form.

Who issues invitations to pickers up? It is the landowner, the shoot captain or the head gamekeeper, not members of the syndicate, guest guns or fellow pickers up. A brace of pheasants in exchange for a day's work is the norm and, with shoot costs escalating, amateur

Head keeper with pickers up, Chipchase Castle.

pickers up who do not expect monetary gain are especially welcome. If you do get paid don't expect a brace of birds as well, although you might get an invitation to the keepers' day at the end of the season. Picking up on a grouse moor is different. With the price of a brace of grouse so high, both from clients who shoot and then from the game dealer, one grouse moor host told me that he couldn't entertain me picking up without pay. Having spent a season previously toiling in the beating line on the grouse moor, I accepted that logic. You earn every penny on the moor even if you only put three brace in the bag.

You have to work at it just like any other job worth doing. Shoots change tenants and sometimes their keepers more frequently than they did even ten years ago. When you are given picking up dates to put in your diary these must be regarded as a serious commitment. Telephoning the night before the shoot to say that you are too busy to come because you haven't finished your Christmas shopping or your partner has a business lunch you don't want to miss, won't do. You have only yourself to blame next time you go along if your pitch has been taken by a business-like fellow in tweeds with three whistles around his neck and a brace of retrievers at each ankle. Picking up in the twenty-first century may have become a sport in its own right, but remember always that the guns call the tune and they enable the show to go on. Without their patronage there would be no day at all. There are rules and we must stick to them. I have always regarded it as a privilege to be invited to work my dogs on private estates. I am sure that you will do so too.

We cannot go picking up without the tools for the job. And the criteria is a good dog. So now let's find the dog.

Chapter 2

<u>The Right Dog</u>

I have had seven working dogs to date during my thirty-five years picking up and only two of those were stars. I would say that ratio is the norm. Certain dogs are better than others in different circumstances, very few are perfect. It is the same with horses. After a lifetime following hounds I can think of only three hunters we have owned which were outstanding with good temperaments and first rate all-round ability. All we can do when we choose a puppy from a litter or try to breed one, is to leave no stone unturned in the pursuit of the qualities we want in our retriever.

Amateur gundog handlers who expect to combine their

Join the beaters on a local shoot and see who owns a good rough shooting dog. Enquire from whom it was bought and ask who trained it.

dogs' activities to embrace both picking up and competing in field trials must be aware that the two disciplines are not always compatible and when you read the chapters in this book about how your retriever will have to work in the shooting field and what we will be expected to do, you will appreciate why this is so. I do know professional trainers who successfully combine the two jobs and take their trials dogs picking up, but they will not be young dogs. We need a dog that we can take picking up as soon as it is ready to begin serious work.

The best advice I can give is to remain dogless for one shooting season yourself and to watch the pickers up at work. You can also watch the guns' dogs too. The man who carries a gun and must spend much of his day at his peg needs a rock-steady retriever and I have nothing but admiration for guns who train their own puppies and achieve this. The qualities we are looking for in our picking up dog are slightly different. We need initiative, a zest for hunting, a good nose, marking ability and control.

For picking up work I would recommend one of the Labrador breed or a Golden Retriever. I did start with a Springer Spaniel, but I live near grouse moors and knew that I would be able to work in that environment. There are good Flatcoat Retrievers and HPR representatives doing excellent work too, but by and large those that are effective are handled by experienced people who know their individual breed. Breeders of gundogs are now producing puppies with such latent ability that to produce a useful working gundog a trainer need do no more than develop those natural gifts of intelligence, nose, mouth and the instinct to retrieve. But remember that if the puppy has an illustrious pedigree with several field trial champions in it designed to increase drive, speed and style in its work then it could be challenging to train. It also depends upon the lifestyle you have to offer the dog, working gundog strains are not particularly restful on the hearth, they need discipline, constant vigilance and a sensible routine. That is why I emphasis that it is wise to watch the other picker uppers' useful dogs. I admit to being greatly influenced in my original choice of a Spaniel because for a whole shooting season I watched two with different owners, working quietly and consistently well. I made enquiries and found, not greatly to my surprise, that they had been trained by the same man, a gamekeeper at Edmundbyers in County Durham. I had no experience and in those days there was minimal help available for a novice wishing to train a young gundog and I was extremely busy with four young children. I bought a two-year-old trained Springer Spaniel bitch from the man, went up to the moors with him on two occasions so that he could show me how to work her and brought my new recruit home. That little dog was a natural – intelligent, biddable and a brilliant retriever. After all these years I remember her with gratitude. Getting the right first dog is so important for a novice picker up. Apart from building the handler's confidence, a useful working partnership opens doors. Word soon gets around the neighbourhood if you and your dog are capable of working quietly, competently and alone for five or six drives putting pricked birds into the game-bag.

It is important to like the breed so if you do fancy, say, a Cocker Spaniel or a Weimaraner then seek out a working strain and go for it. After all you are going to have to look at the dog for the next ten years and the relationship between man and dog must be built on mutual respect. You will work better with a dog you feel close to rather than one you feel you should have, because of the dictates of fashion.

There are basically two choices. Either buy in a trained dog which will be eighteen months to two years old, from a professional trainer or perhaps a keeper, or buy a puppy either to send away for training or to train yourself. There are other permutations. The sporting press sometimes offer young dogs part-trained or you may inherit a retriever which you feel could be guided into a useful picker up but for the purposes of this book we'll stick to the first two options. Whatever you decide to do, check the young dog's parentage carefully, indeed I would say if

Labradors are a popular choice of breed for picking up work.

at all possible see both parents at work in the shooting field, especially the dam, or speak to someone who has. It will be too late when halfway through the season and having problems with a miscreant you are then told that your young hopeful's sire was the wildest canine ever seen in the county. Buying locally is usually the wisest option if at all possible.

There is no need to feel ashamed of buying a trained dog especially if you are a busy person. The ideal is a dog which has had one season's experience in the shooting field. Have some lessons in how to handle him. It will cost money, but can be regarded as an investment, a good picking up dog should give years of satisfaction. The secret of a good gundog which remains consistently reliable is solid groundwork in that essential discipline – obedience. It isn't everyone who can instil that.

If you have the time to give to a puppy and wish to train it yourself there is no reason why you should not be successful. There is a lot of knowledgeable help available today and the amateur trainer can find private tuition and gundog classes in the form of weekly lessons or weekend courses in almost all parts of Britain. For the purposes of this book I have attended training courses in Dorset, Yorkshire, Northumberland and Scotland with my current young dog. Every trainer knew what I needed in a picking up dog. But gundog puppies are not bred for this specific purpose so when you are faced with a litter of eight-week-old pups any one of them might train on into a gun's dog, a trials dog or a good picker up. It's a lottery and background and breeding are the criteria. If the pups have steady working parents they should all turn into good game-finders so try and pick the one in the litter which appeals to you personally.

Dog or bitch? A bitch comes into season twice a year and can therefore cause timing problems, a dog can be a nuisance all year round. Given the opportunity to do so, a dog will be more likely to stray. A bitch is softer and easier to train, a dog will face cover more boldly – these are truisms, yet also false. It depends upon the individual dog. If you already have a dog or a bitch in the family think carefully before opting to have a different sex on the place.

Chapter 3

<u>In The Doghouse</u>

W hether the new dog is an eight-week-old puppy or a young adult when you bring it home a sensible routine, and code of manners will have to be worked out. This book is not a training manual, but guidance is needed. For those important first six to eight months the advice I give for a puppy applies equally to an older dog integrating into the family.

Home rules for gundogs. 'Oh dear! Are you expecting me to stay here. . . ?'

A young family need not, necessarily, spoil your gundog for its work in the field. This is too often an excuse offered by the man, or woman, whose own shortcomings have reduced a responsive and potentially biddable dog into an unco-operative one. Nevertheless, those of us who have to house and entertain an exuberant young gundog, sometimes two, for the long six months of the close season are faced with a challenge which we must take steps to understand. A bored dog will readily pick up bad habits even in the confines of the home policies. Wild walks are pure joy for a gundog, particularly a spaniel. Prevention is better than a cure so avoid the temptations offered by local gamey smells. Once the hunting habit is acquired and the dog learns to get his head down among the delicious smells in the hedgerows it is extremely difficult for the layman to break it. The dog should only hunt game under supervision. So choose boring walks where there are no temptations, however tedious this may

A disastrous episode – never let children throw dummies for your gundog.

become and then the dog can enjoy reasonable freedom to exercise. Reserve the interesting gamey walks for training sessions. Dogs are not as intelligent as humans, they live entirely for the moment so if the walk is boring he will not be mentally comparing it with where he would rather be.

A wise friend of mine once told me to avoid over-use of the lead with a picking-up dog, and never to give my dog an order which I was not certain of being able to enforce. It was good advice. Eye contact should be substituted for a lead, the idea is to build up a thread between you. Dogs are basically servile creatures and enjoy being willing servants so the idea is to establish contact using the eye and the voice. You have to continually work at this and never get slack about manners and obedience. If I put the lead on and under certain circumstances I do so, then my dog's dependence upon me is broken and she no longer has to answer to me for her actions. Watch a good trainer and you can see him maintaining eye contact all the time with his pupils.

If any order is not strictly enforced, it is best not to give it. We have all seen guns telling their dog to 'sit' whilst talking to friends on the shoot. The dog obeys and remains momentarily in situ but within a short time has risen from his haunches and moved away. Engaged in conversation, his owner either permits the lapse or does not notice. Dogs are not fools and know when their master is distracted. In the shooting field, when I know some of the guns I have a chat. One can hardly be churlish and spend the whole time chastising the dogs, so I do put a lead on if I feel my young dog or for that matter the old one, might take advantage of my inattention. At home I keep words of command like 'heel' and 'sit' to be used only on the shooting field and never allow the family to abuse them, the same applies to the whistle. I keep that strictly for use on training walks. Amateurs have a tendency to use too many words when training a young dog. I have been way back in the woods picking up with novice handlers and listened to a string of contradictory orders and exhortations which must sound like Russian to their dog – rather like the Englishman travelling abroad who is under the impression that all natives understand English, provided it is shouted loud enough. This principle must not be applied to gundogs. Your dog's hearing is sensitive and frequent exhortation when giving a command only results in confusion in the animal's consciousness. One of the most valuable lessons which I learnt when I went on one training course for pickers up was how sloppy my vocabulary to my young dog had become without me noticing it.

Six words should be all you need for a picking-up dog. 'Heel' which, once learnt, I change to a hiss 'sss-t' a sound less disturbing for game or irritating for the guns to hear. 'Sit', 'wait' (use 'stay' if you prefer) 'hie-lost', 'over' for walls and dykes and 'steady' which is useful in bringing on a young enthusiastic dog working too fast and tending to over-run a line. Sitting well back from the guns in a peat hag or in a wood you can chat to your dogs in any language you like but that is only for their ears. I have a whistle but rarely use it picking up.

Never take your young picking-up dog out riding. I have two gundogs and a hunter to exercise but do not combine the two because I know it will spell long term disaster for the dogs' work in the shooting field. In the saddle when I am concentrating primarily on my horse they quickly learn that I am in no position to exert control. They slide off into the hedgerows at every opportunity.

If you find it more convenient to have your picking up dog living indoors with the family, then he or she must learn a code of acceptable behaviour. Commonsense will dictate because, in so many ways, the education of young intelligent dogs is much like the training of children. The dogs must be taught to go straight to their baskets and to stay there when it is inconvenient to have them underfoot. If there are other dogs in the family be careful about leaving them all unsupervised in the garden. Whippets and terriers especially are born ringleaders when it comes to illicit jaunts and you must not have your budding picking up dog getting into the habit of slipping off to look for rabbits with his friends.

Car drill is important and we do not all have cages for our retrievers. I teach my dogs to wait before getting in and out of my car from an early age. It is infuriating to have muddy, wet dogs crowding unbidden into the estate vehicle or onto the trailer before the handlers have taken their seats. Some drives are near roads and it is dangerous if a dog leaps out as soon as the door of the vehicle is opened. When I arrive at the shoot rendezvous in the morning I open the estate car boot, but have trained the dogs to sit quietly while I get my coat on and greet friends: a few moments of control in what is an exciting moment for them. This gives me the upper hand and hopefully puts them into the right frame of mind for the day.

Car drill is important and dogs must be taught to wait before getting in or out of the car.

Chapter 4

First Lessons for the Picking Up Dog

I t is for the lost birds that we are training our picking up dog, not those that lie in the open which you can gather yourself, or the guns' dogs can. It is nose work we are introducing our retriever to, not guess work so I use the dummy sparingly. I think that many of the ineffective dogs out today owe their failure as reliable pickers up because of too much dummy work. Gundogs are so bred that eighty per cent are natural retrievers, perhaps I have been lucky but I have not yet had one which did not take to the job with alacrity. On seeing dummies puppies can become bored, and I think that is when they pick up irritating habits, such as circling the handler, instead of giving the retrieve correctly. Once the puppy has to hunt for its reward, the boredom question is unlikely to arise.

I have found an older dog invaluable in teaching a youngster to face cover, because a picking up dog must learn to go into brambles, rushy dykes, down steep slopes and into any undergrowth however thick, if its nose tells it that that is where the stricken bird had hidden. I teach this under supervision on our training walks. As the young dog gains confidence watch for signs of independence and correct accordingly because rabbits abound now in hedgerows and dykes and any tendency in the puppy to hunt for itself must be checked. Vigilance and discipline are the criteria in the dog and master relationship so the youngster must never taste the joys of illicit chasing or turning a deaf ear and breaking the rules. Gundogs are naturally servile and the happiest are those which are under control and serving master correctly. It is a unique companionship and there must be mutual respect so that each respects the others' expertise and builds on it.

Introduce the dog to stock as soon as it is five or six months old, this means cattle, sheep and domestic fowls. There is one stand where I pick up at Preston Towers behind a cottage where bantams scratch and strut within yards of us. I nearly had a fit when I first took a young dog there and she emerged from a bramble bush with an indignant, squawking bantam cock. Mercifully I was able to release him with nothing more than ruffled feathers. It taught me a salutary lesson. Sheep will run at minimal disturbance from dogs, and bullocks are inquisitive and take the opposite stance by circling the dogs. So I take the young dog deliberately near stock at an impressionable age and sit her as soon as they move. The dog quickly gets bored, understands what I'm getting at and ignores stock for the rest of her working life.

On the average day picking up on a shoot a dog can find itself faced with a variety of obstacles – walls, cattle grids, streams and the bane of the gundog owner's life, barbed-wire fences. The latter are a real hazard especially those with a barbed-wire strand along the top. I carry a game-bag and lay this along the place I wish the dog to jump and I teach this lesson early in field work although it isn't always practical to use it. I also use it myself, so my plus fours are not torn. When we are walking between drives on the shoot I like to have my dogs 'wait' at every gate or fence for the order to proceed. It is infuriating to have them feathering busily across the next field when you are either waiting with a group of guns to file through a gate or climbing over a fence or wall. On every shoot we see adult gundogs being lifted over fences, coaxed between wires and heaved over stiles. The whole party is held up while the dog is persuaded to use his initiative, although you will likely see the same dog later in the day going over and through anything in pursuit of a runner. Take the pup on interesting walks in the home policies where he will meet natural obstacles and teach him how to cope with them. Whenever possible I leave

The gundog on the shoot is constantly beset by awkward obstacles.

the youngster either to follow an older dog or to work it out for herself. I try not to help unless it is strictly necessary. Most dogs love jumping, start small and avoid timber and walls until legs get stronger. A good clean jumper is an enormous asset for the picker up. Cattle grids are common in Northumberland so on training walks, I teach the dogs never to try and run across. They must look for a way round and they quickly understand the drill.

Some breeds take readily to water, others are more hesitant. The finest retriever in water I have seen was a Chesapeake Bay, not surprising as the breed is the champion of ducking dogs, one has even swum the English Channel. Spaniels have the edge over Labradors in water but, as a general rule, if swimming is introduced correctly at an impressionable age there will not be problems. That is provided you take care that the puppy

Introducing a young dog to water.

does not get a fright in water because then she will be reluctant to face it again. Unless you have an older dog to encourage the puppy, put on wellies and wade in yourself. It is a question of building up confidence. Dogs have different ways of entering water, some leap in boldly, others paddle sedately, you can't change that. Once the pup has begun to relax and enjoy her plodge in the stream, I throw a stick for her for one or two lessons and then graduate to the dummy. Avoid early water training in severe winter months because it can be very cold. Once a measure of competence has been acquired I stop dummy work entirely in the water and only take the dogs for a relaxing swim every day in the summer if I can spare the time. My Dachshunds refuse to wet a paw but the gundogs love visiting the stream. Labradors and Golden Retrievers have a habit of retrieving their bird from water and having gained dry land, will drop it to shake themselves before bringing it in to the handler. Some field trial judges will mark a dog down for this. In my experience, no half-decent retriever would drop a runner to do this but if they do pause for a shake and then bring in the dead bird it is of little consequence.

The best picking up dogs I know did not come to their best until they were at least three years old. I am sure that this is because their respective trainers 'made haste slowly' and did not overface their dog as a puppy. Gundogs have such latent ability today that in the majority of cases, training is a matter of guidance and it is easy to rush things. My heart sinks when I see a puppy under a year old picking up in the field under battle conditions. Yes, some people do take them out at such a young age. A dog will never be so steady as in its first season before it has learnt the wiles and deceptions of running in or poaching a bird from under another dog's nose. When you do take out your new recruit make sure he only works on unseen birds for the whole of his first season.

Finally some basic training for the handler. Before aspiring to become a picker up you must learn how to dispatch game humanely. Whacking the bird on the head with a stick is a hit or miss job and if you are working several dogs who arrive with runners all at the same time this method is simply not practical, especially for a woman. The best way is a sharp twist to break the bird's neck, once you've got the knack you'll never lose it so get someone experienced to teach you how. Young grouse can have the head snapped off quite easily so be careful with them, a wounded cock pheasant takes more skill. I can now kill wounded birds with a twist of the wrist but there is more to it than a simple whirling round. The weight of the bird's body is used against the firmly held neck and head of the bird to cause a fracture which is instant. A wounded partridge can be instantly killed by a sharp trifling blow on the head. Not so the woodcock, prick him immediately behind the pinion joint under the wing and he will instantly expire. Correctly dispatching game is a knack and with practice you will get it right. As a last resort buy a purpose-made game dispatcher.

Chapter 5

Training Courses for Pickers Up

With the joys and trials of being a member of a picking up team becoming almost as popular as shooting itself, courses for novice gundog handlers are arranged by professional trainers in various parts of Britain. I took my young Labrador along to find out more. I knew that we would have to work hard and expected that to some degree my dog and I would benefit, but what I hadn't expected was how much we would enjoy ourselves. These courses are a mix of hard work and socialising. 'I like my guests to go away from a course at my place feeling that they have had a holiday and made new friends as well as having improved their dogs' technique and their own understanding of the role of the picker up,' said Walter Harrison who runs courses in Dorset. 'A relaxed atmosphere helps the learning

Picking up class for amateur gundog handlers.

Course for pickers up in Dumfriesshire.

experience.'

The emphasis on every course is on training the handler as much as the dog, a formula which has proved popular with novice pickers up who want to refresh themselves as well as their dogs before the shooting season begins. If our dogs ran riot and chased after a rabbit, we had to leg it after them and reprimand on the spot. The best courses are run like simulated shoot days.

On the first course I attended my dread was that all the other dogs on the course would be budding field trial candidates with po-faced owners who would frown at our bungling efforts. I couldn't have been more wrong. In every case they were an enthusiastic group, both men and women, mostly with a young dog (but in a few cases, a delinquent old one) anxious to bring out the potential in their dogs so that they could make themselves useful on local shoots. A few were interested in getting involved in working tests, some just wanted to find out whether their canine displayed any aptitude for field work. There usually is a preponderance of Labradors, Golden Retrievers and Spaniels but there were also Setters, Flatcoat Retrievers, hunt, point retrieve breeds and lesser known ones, like the useful Chesapeake Bay. You learn a lot from watching the others. These courses are run during the close season for game shooting, with the occasional advanced follow-up course arranged in late September and October.

The first course I attended was a salutary lesson in how I had been getting things wrong. My signals to my dog were abysmal. 'Take those gloves off,' admonished George Ridley, the trainer. 'Your dog can't see what you're getting at . . .' Well of course she couldn't and as a result she only listened when it suited her. I took the gloves off and she began to take my signals seriously. My 'stop' whistle had become almost non-existent so that was sharpened up. On the best courses, guns shoot live game with Spaniels flushing rabbits, students 'hup' their dogs and send them to retrieve on command: marvellous steadiness practice. On one advanced course I attended in October my dog retrieved her first woodcock.

One lady had a Clumber Spaniel with a distaste for water retrieving. 'He comes from a line of Crufts winners. But he shows natural ability,' she said. 'He enjoys working, but we have streams into which pheasants often fall where I go to pick up and he isn't keen on getting his feet wet. I want guidelines on how to handle him without breaking his spirit.' By the end of that excellent four-day training course in Dorset, the Clumber was enthusiastically retrieving dummies from a small lake.

Clients are encouraged to talk about any worries that they have, with trainers giving advice on persuading diffident canine pupils to face thick cover, and to jump walls and dykes. Understanding every lesson is the basic

Pupil under the supervision of a trainer.

Class in progress: George Ridley instructing with Andrew Wilkinson in the foreground.

necessity for a successful partnership – Obedience, and this included correct walking to heel.

Most trainers who run these courses will board clients' dogs free of charge for the duration of a residential course, a bonus for a Geordie like me who has had to travel the length and breadth of Britain checking out the best courses. I always took a dog along, you have to be involved at grass roots level to assess potential. Advice is given about etiquette on the shooting field, what to wear and how to behave as a member of a picking up team. Courses may be home-based when you live with the

31

Game Conservancy gundog training day with John Halstead at Newby Hall, Yorkshire. This picture shows a water retrieve demonstration.

trainer on a bed and breakfast basis, or the course is based on hotel accommodation. I have seen complete novices loaned a trained dog for a day's tuition. This would not suit me but it might be worthwhile to find out whether gundog work appeals before taking the irrevocable step of buying a dog for yourself.

Should you find it difficult to spare the time, or cash, to attend a residential course make enquiries about local training classes held on a weekly or monthly basis in your neighbourhood. The people to ask are the gundog clubs in the region, the Kennel Club has all addresses and telephone numbers. Professional gundog trainers all give one-to-one handler tuition where in-depth work is achieved, useful if you have a potential problem but expensive on a long-term basis, around £25 to £30 for a 45 minute session. Weekly and residential courses have been born out of these private lessons as a logical extension. Whatever course you consider, personal recommendation is the criteria. There are some duff 'trainers' about today who call themselves professionals who cannot manage their own dogs on the shoot, never mind teaching novices how to handle theirs. So make enquiries from past clients before committing yourself.

The British Association for Shooting and Conservation and the Game Conservancy host training days in different parts of Britain. These courses are concerned primarily with practical work in the shooting field and not with working tests or trial work. I have found these day courses extremely helpful and all the ones I attended were led by a top-class gundog trainer with venues well located throughout the country. The emphasis is on dog management in the field using the dog for picking up or as an aid to the gun, leaning towards educating the handler rather than the dog.

'On these training days we do not intend to produce a reliable gundog in one day but to show the handler how, by following the right sequence with proven methods, he can correctly train and control his gundog,' BASC's education department told me. It is not necessary to take

Well done! A pupil hands over a successful retrieve.

a dog, but advantageous to do so. Average cost is £40 for the day and you take your own lunch. On the training days which I attended aspects in training from basic obedience to retrieving and, in the case of Spaniels hunting up were covered but they do not try to emulate the more in-depth courses run over several days or weeks offered by professional trainers and gundog societies.

If there is not one of these day courses in your area, why not contact your local regional BASC or Game Conservancy director or chairman and offer to organise one for them? That is what I did in Northumberland. The day was oversubscribed. It did take a degree of planning, mainly circulating local gundog societies, sending notices to the sporting press and fixing up the village hall for the lunch break (a garage would do at a pinch for this) but BASC supported me. I joined in the course on the day,

Join a gundog training class. Peter Chambers (right) with a Northumberland group.

George Ridley giving instruction at Deanraw Gundog and Handler Centre in Northumberland.

with a young dog.

The Dorset branch of the Game Conservancy organises a day for potential pickers up and young dogs, hosted by Randal MacGregor at his first-time-through pheasant shoot day. This is a wonderful day for potential pickers up to go out under instruction on a fully-fledged shoot day. Gay Hanbury of Dorchester, one of the instructors and organisers of these days, told me: 'We start the course with an evening in the pub with a short lecture on picking up. Everything is covered from a check list of what to take, questions to ask before you arrive (lunch, pay, etc.), to manners on arrival, what to ask the keeper, checks to be made with other pickers up, checking on release pens, next drives, etc. There are always a lot of questions from anxious participants. On the day itself there are four instructors and sixteen trainees. Hopefully, the guns do not bring dogs but even if they do it is quite a good lesson in how to cope with guns' dogs. I take an experienced dog myself for runners because many of the trainees' dogs have never picked a bird at all. Each group stands back from the guns, not in line but not too far back so that they are able to see what is going on. We hope for not too many birds down, not too far away to start with, although the last drive of the day involves sweeping a wood afterwards, but it is likely the instructors' dogs will do the bulk of the real work. The trainees will usually get a bird each per drive to pick up which is plenty for young dogs and it is very rewarding to get the beginners retrieving confidently by the end of the day.

At the time of writing this report, Dorset is the only county holding a day like this but more may soon follow because the sporting press has given our days a lot of coverage. It is best if potential trainees telephone the

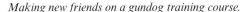

Making new friends on a gundog training course.

Game Conservancy to find out about courses planned for the current year. We are always oversubscribed and only take dogs which have achieved a reasonable standard of training already. Dogs out of control are sent back to the vehicles, but this is not a field trial and I am quite happy for a dog to be on a lead as long as necessary.'

The cost is £20 for members of the Game Conservancy and £25 (non-members) the profit going to Game Conservancy funds.

Chapter 6

<u>Etiquette in the Field</u>

It is now time to graduate to actually working in the field as a picker up. Your dog should be ready to hunt and retrieve under supervision, on the real thing. Here I reiterate that invitations to pick up on a shoot come only from landowners, or shoot managers, or from a head gamekeeper, not from a gun in the shoot. Prove your worth in the beating line if necessary. Occasionally, a picker up who has worked several years on a shoot can recommend a novice. You could also accompany a gun (your husband, partner or a friend?), keep a low profile, note how many pickers up there are on the shoot and roughly where they stand and at the end of the day make discreet enquiries as to whether there is space for a new recruit on the team. Your dog meanwhile will have been behaving in exemplary fashion. As in so many spheres of working life it is a matter of networking and starting on the bottom rung, in this case the beating line, if necessary.

The first day for a picker up is never easy. You have to learn the geography of the shoot, how the drives work, where the guns stand and how and where the birds fly. Much will depend upon the direction of the prevailing wind on the day, so having spent one or two days on the shoot you may think you understand the estate layout and how each drive is organised only to find that next time you go along the wind is in a different direction and plans have changed. One trainer suggested that a novice on a new shoot might find it useful to take a pad and pencil and, whilst waiting for the birds to come over, to sketch a circle indicating where the guns stand and another circle representing your own position. Each time a bird falls, either dead or crippled, you mark the position with an X. This sounds simple but I wouldn't find it practical because I can't fumble with pencil and paper whilst watching my dogs and the action. On a big day with dozens of pheasants coming over you need to concentrate and keep your wits about you, otherwise you miss marking a suspect bird or your dog takes advantage and slips off to work unbidden. Anyway, keepers change drives from season to season, sometimes from one day to the next so a sketch would probably soon turn out to be obsolete.

Wear comfortable, waterproof clothing and on the grouse moor, avoid bright colours, i.e. a jazzy jacket. Jeans and trainers are impractical, wear wellingtons or short boots except for very hot days in the heather when trainers could be worn if you are working as a beater. Should you like to carry a stick, holly is harder than hazel. Cut it in winter, when the sap is low and let it dry slowly in a shed or, better still, hang it from the beams on a ceiling with the heaviest end down. If you use ash, choose one with a good root growth because this could make a natural handle. I like to carry a game-bag, not only to put dead birds into, but also to carry a spare lead, and my waterproof hat. If you don't wish to be encumbered by a bag, there are handy game carriers on the market which can go in a pocket. When you start to fill them with birds, they go over the shoulder. Take your own packed lunch unless specifically told not to do so, a day without sustenance is not recommended. Keep it simple unless you have your own vehicle all day. The shoot manager or head keeper will usually supply one or two vehicles for the pickers up. Sometimes a picker up likes to be independent and use his, or her, own transport and it does give you a measure of freedom if you do this, you can spend time looking for a lost bird after the guns have moved on to the next drive. The host and his keeper cannot have the guns hanging about because of a missing picker up but, in my experience, it is rare to be left behind, it has not yet happened to me. I don't use my own vehicle but use the estate transport or double up with another picker up. Once you learn the estate layout, get to know the natives and how each drive is organised everything becomes easier. It is often possible to walk from one drive to the next so you can stay behind to find an elusive bird and then catch up but if you intend to do this, tell someone reliable so no one is kept waiting for you.

During my first season picking up on the grouse moor I got peppered with shot. It was my own fault entirely and it taught me a salutary lesson. You should be within 200 yards of the butts or pegs, there is no point in being close, you are not there to pick up birds around the guns, unless you have been told to do so, in which case it is safer to stand in the line, especially on a partridge shoot. There are sometimes instances when you need to stand in line with the guns because there is a main road or a river or some other obstacle which does not allow a picker up to stand well back. Do not be tempted to choose a new pitch and to crouch down and hide if you are within range. This is not only dangerous but extremely alarming for the gun who spots you popping up unexpectedly.

Arrive before time at the meeting place and leave the dogs in your vehicle until you are organised with coat and boots on and instructions received. It is bad manners to have excited dogs weaving around the guns' legs and relieving themselves in your host's yard. If you need to

Dogs should be taught to wait for an order before they leave the vehicle.

ask the keeper what he wants you to do, which vehicle you will travel in or who is in charge of the pickers up, time must be allowed for this before he gets involved with his boss and the guests or clients. If you are handed over to a veteran picker up, put yourself in his hands, keep your mouth shut and stand where he tells you to and don't wander about. A new recruit can count on being given the less productive corners, the old timers will keep the hot spots for themselves but wild birds are unpredictable and always keep one guessing. After several seasons on the shoot you will have learnt the drives, at least to some degree and will know instinctively where to stand to make yourself useful. Never forget that picking up is a team effort, you are all there to pull together and not to compete for the most productive corners.

Occasionally a picker up may be asked to act as a stop in the pheasant cover or on the grouse moor. I always enjoy this. It is a chance to enjoy a different view of the terrain and valuable for the dogs to have a different role. Time between drives must not be spent socialising with the guns, however well you may know them. If you are doing your job properly you will be busy working your dogs searching for the slain or comparing progress with another picker up, or even a sharp-eyed beater.

Join the guns for lunch if you have been invited to do so otherwise muck in with beaters and pickers-up. It is prudent to resist liberal resource to the cherry brandy proffered by a kind host or a friendly gun. The wind may be biting and the frost keen but you have to keep your wits about you and your voice in low key. The shooting field is still male dominated and the girls won't always find it easy to find a secluded spot to use as a loo, another good reason to restrict liquid intake.

Finally, I always thank my host at the end of every day picking up for allowing me to come and help. The days when veteran pickers up could behave like *prima donnas* are over and those of us invited to help should regard it as a privilege to be invited to do so.

Chapter 7

<u>Covert Days</u>

A usual plan adopted by gamekeepers organising a pheasant, or partridge, shoot is to begin near the estate boundary and to drive the birds homewards, placing guns at the end of each covert in turn and pushing the birds over them towards ground they habitually frequent. But one keeper I spoke to about this considered that driving homewards seldom contributed to satisfactory sport on the estate he looked after. He preferred to force his birds as far as possible away from their customary resorts in order that they might return in defiance of all obstacles. This is confusing for the picker up trying to learn the form because, although the pattern

George Roberts on a partridge day, Gurston Down, Wiltshire.

Pickers up receive instructions from the keeper on a pheasant shoot.

of the drives on different shoots may have nothing to do with him, nevertheless we must learn where to stand to be efficient.

'I'm difficult to work for,' one man admitted. 'I make a plan before a shoot but there are many times I make up the day as I go along. Sometimes the wind changes unexpectedly or there has been some disturbance near a covert so I alter a drive. I expect my pickers up to be observant, alert to last minute changes and to get themselves into safe positions where they can be most effective.' In other words we sometimes have to be mind readers. The majority of regular pickers up live within reasonable distance of the pheasant or partridge shoots they work on and can, with permission, visit the estate occasionally during the off season and note work going on there. Coverts may be felled, new areas replanted, rearing pens moved and different crops grown on the fields, all relevant factors which can change the pattern of a shoot day. Things don't stay the same from year to year. On some pheasant shoots the drives are close together which means the picker up must have a dog which is totally obedient otherwise there will be danger of ruining

---

Driven pheasant.

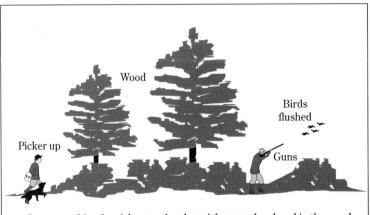

Correct position for picker up. Another picker may be placed in the wood, especially if the gun has no dog.

not only the next drive but others as well. Pheasants quickly learn the form and make themselves scarce when there is disturbance. The common pattern on a pheasant shoot is for guns to stand between two woods with the pickers up standing inside the wood to which the birds are being driven and behind the guns with one just forward from the tree line to pick wounded birds before they reach cover. This plan is adopted so that strong unshot birds which land in the cover can run on through the wood. At the end of the drive the pickers up move slowly forward together, not coming in at angles, thus allowing fit birds to escape through the line rather than being confused and then 'pegged' by dogs. Either stand in line with the guns, a common practice on a partridge shoot, or well back. That means far enough back that it is rare to go back for a bird, and you come forward to retrieve. Having decided where you are going to stand, put your dogs on sit and keep marking every bird to the best of your ability. If there is a release pen in the wood it is likely the pheasants will make for this, so a picker up standing in or near the pen can quickly spot and deal with crippled birds as they land. When the drive is over and not before, the picker up moves into action by sending a dog for the strongest runner. This is the criteria but not a rule, because in certain circumstances collecting a bird during a drive is permissible provided the dog will be tracking away from the action. If I see a winged cock hit the ground and streak for the nearest forbidden covert I will send a reliable dog to collect. This makes sense. We have all had experience of the strong runner we have marked but which, half an hour later, the combined efforts of your good retrievers fail to find. It happens to the best pickers up.

Now we come to the essence of good picking up – game sense. This means instinctively knowing whether a bird is going to run or not, using the wind and habitat to your dogs' advantage and instinctively knowing where a bird is likely to tuck in and hide. This knowledge comes with experience. No one can teach it, you have to get out there and get involved, try and make as few mistakes as possible and watch the experienced pickers up and their dogs to see how they do it. When it comes to the crunch that is the only way to learn. Experience brings confidence in marking birds, noting contours of hillock, ditch and scree so that you can go straight to the fall when the drive is over. A few birds mustered and brought to hand bring confidence to both dog and handler.

An observant picker up will quickly learn to identify wounded birds still airborne – their flight is erratic, they have dropped a leg or their landing is clumsy. A few species, especially grouse, may 'tower' which means flying directly upwards before falling to the ground. These last are almost always dead and can be extraordinarily elusive to find. Nevertheless almost without exception I do find them, because it is relatively easy to mark the exact fall of these birds on a grouse moor. An experienced dog can become as skilled as his master at learning the drill, my nine-year-old Labrador can sense a wounded bird even though I may think that it

The picker up waits for the action.

is unharmed. I watch her body language to recognise the ones that have been wounded. She gives me a knowing look and I let her off, trusting my dog's instinct. Almost every time she returns with a crippled bird. When a bird is mortally hit, its head flies back and there is a puff of feathers from the front of the body but if the rear end flips it is likely the shot has hit too far back to kill instantly. A bird with a dropped leg is one to collect, it will scarcely be able to move from the fall area. A young bird can trip up on landing and is likely to be only tired. With experience, you soon become clever at remembering where a bird fell and mentally marking the place using trees, telegraph poles, patches of rushes, fences, walls, rowan bushes, rocks and even bramble bushes. When you see a runner hobbling into covert it can be heart-stopping, but nine times out of ten a wounded bird will tuck in as soon as it reaches sanctuary and can be picked later. Hen birds are particularly prone to crouch and hide.

Birds that are difficult to find attract other eager dog handlers quick to throw their dogs into the search. Ask the picker up or the gun already working his dogs if they would like help. Too many dogs running about an area can confuse the scent and is distracting, especially for a young dog. If it seems to be becoming a free-for-all I call my dogs out of the pack and look for somewhere else to make ourselves useful.

If a gun has a dog, he will want to use it for the birds around his peg, or butt; there are some guns who like to pick their birds by hand. If you have not had the opportunity to speak to the gun concerned before the drive then wait until he has moved away before working the area to find birds left behind. Guns in a syndicate shoot get to know the pickers up and strike up a working relationship with them so that each can help the other. I always take the trouble to report if I have found a runner and I have yet to meet the gun who is nonchalant about whether the woodcock he shot has been found. If I cannot find a specific bird I say so, or tell the keeper at the lunch break or at the end of the day. There are men who continually send the pickers up after mythical birds they think they hit and I know one contemporary of mine who plods off dutifully to pretend to search for the bird and later tells the gun, sometimes the keeper too, that he had found it 'stone dead'. He has been known to hold up a bird from a previous drive as proof of his dedication. I will not be a party to this because the gun is simply being encouraged to continue sending long-suffering pickers up over the horizon on fruitless searches. If I have seen the bird myself and know it to be unscathed and over the horizon I'm inclined to say so. You need to use commonsense here, it might be churlish to doubt the word of your host's chief guest. Many guns are accurate markers and extremely helpful. With experience you soon get to know who can give a reliable mark.

Dogs have different ways of hunting covert after a drive. Some instinctively range large areas whilst others hoover every bush and tussock in a restricted area but do not cover so much ground. I know one strong-minded Clumber Spaniel which will not leave an area until he has found his bird, a grand little dog which works close and thoroughly. The ideal is to have two dogs, each with a different system of hunting and then they won't miss much but they must be obedient, under control. A 'wild' dog is a disaster and can easily ruin future drives. As the owner of such a culprit your name will be blackened however good your other dogs. In the southern counties there are inevitably many drives on shoots which are uncomfortably close to busy highways and a wilful dog would be a disaster here.

One friend of ours visits his family's shoot on big days to help pick up with a large, panting Labrador on a string. I know the dog well and it was once a useful retriever but is now, alas, out of control. 'I know he would improve if I could come out more often,' sighed my friend. Alas, dogs do not necessarily improve with more lively birds to retrieve, rather than less and neither do their handlers. The moral of this story is that if you do wish to be taken seriously as a reliable picker up and if you run into problems with a dog, pocket your pride, ask for advice, visit a trainer for help, make every effort to get things right. But do not take the miscreant picking up again until you have him organised. We all make mistakes. Years ago I had a two-year-old Springer Spaniel with the right credentials, but too much *chutzpah* for her own good. 'She's ready to spoil,' said the keeper on a neighbouring grouse moor who sold her to me at ten months old. I was not a novice and the dog worked well the season after I bought her for the first three weeks picking up on the grouse moor. Then she started to behave like a moron, picking up birds and dropping them, deaf to the whistle, rioting on rabbits. She distracted my other dogs and took all my attention so that the other two got jealous and

A good return.

wilful. Things were going seriously wrong – had I started her too young on live game, and were we beyond help? I cancelled engagements and enrolled on a one-day gundog training course organised by BASC. This turned out to be a learning experience for me as much as for the Spaniel. By the end of the day she was concentrating, looking to me for directions, retrieving a dummy correctly to hand. For the first time during the previous two months I felt that she was anxious to get things right. During the lunch break, the trainer and I thrashed out problems. After that I took things more slowly and that Spaniel subsequently did turn out to be a reliable picking up dog.

Find out how you will know when the drive is over. A lull in shooting may only be a temporary pause in proceedings and not the signal to start working your dog. Watch the guns, the end of the line with one man in view is all you need to be able to see to learn the state of play, or a fellow picker up with a better view may be able to give you a signal. The majority of shoots now signal the end of a drive with two blasts. An intelligent dog picks up the vibes within one season and knows as soon as he hears the horn that he can start work. He must do this however, only when he receives a signal from his handler.

Chapter 8
A Grouse in the Hand

Picking up grouse is one of life's plum jobs. I have started all my young dogs picking up work on the grouse moor and find that the relatively short ground cover encourages them to get their heads down and use their noses. It is good for the handler too, because you can see your dog working almost all the time. If you get the chance to pick up on a grouse moor even if it is only standing with a gun and retrieving around the butts,

Northumberland grouse moor.

don't miss the opportunity. Unlike all other forms of shooting driven birds, the host on a grouse moor lays on an elaborate programme at considerable expense and involving many employees, because he wants his grouse killed. Sometimes a shoot manager of a pheasant day does not want all his birds killed and will organise things with this in mind. With grouse, the criteria is that the best possible bag be shot.

Ideally, take an experienced retriever with a youngster for the first outing for grouse. The bird makes a very good retrieve for a young dog because of the tight structure of feathers but it is a relatively small mouthful and can encourage an enthusiastic canine to seize it too firmly. This can lead to an aggressive retrieving attitude so I have always been careful for the first few days to send my proven dog to fetch and when there is a lull in proceedings, for example at the lunch break, I set up a retrieve lesson with a cool grouse in the heather and send the dog into the wind to collect. Picking up grouse triggers an unfortunate tendency in some handlers to volubly exhort their dogs to try harder in the form of a stream of anxious commands telling them to 'seek', 'hie lost' and 'get on' which makes a fool of the dog which becomes frantic with anxiety at being unable to find the bird. It also makes the handler look inefficient and foolish. Try to remain calm and leave the dog alone, encouraging and directing only when necessary. If he can't find the grouse then it is too difficult at present. On a grouse moor, more than in any other picking up scenario, it is necessary to let the dog range in the area of the fall using his own initiative. It is quite different to picking up pheasants, to a certain extent you have to let your dog hunt without direction, no grouse moor manager likes to see time wasted on his team handling their dogs onto marked slain birds. Yes, it does ruin dogs for working tests and trials, but for those of us who enjoy working in the few wide open spaces still left to us today, picking up grouse on our lovely heather-covered moors is immensely satisfying work.

Scent can be difficult on a grouse moor, especially in very warm weather – which it is often in August. What looks like a carpet of glorious purple as far as you can see may be a nightmare for the dogs. Pollen is a fine powdery substance, consisting of numerous miniscule grains which end up adhering to the mucous linings of your dog's nose and this diminishes his sense of smell. All the dogs will be affected on a day like this, including those used for pointing birds as well as retrieving them. On the whole I would say that these drive conditions are outnumbered by the days when scent is good.

Grouse moors are not docile, gentle mounds of short heather. They can be steep in places and the ling thick in patches, there will be burnt areas covered with gnarled, twisted stalks which tear socks and scratch boots. Try to walk like a Highlander not lifting feet higher than necessary, thus conserving energy. It can be hot and debilitating walking through heather in humid conditions and miserably cold and damp when it is raining which it often does in late summer and early autumn in the

Grouse moor work.

northern uplands. It can be pouring with rain at nine in the morning and hot, sunny and windless by mid-afternoon. But in my experience, the good days outnumber the bad ones. Most burns and peaty bogs can be jumped over or splodged through quickly enough to avoid a soak. I find that wellingtons are too heavy and ankle height waterproof boots are ideal. Barbour-type jackets are also too heavy on the grouse moor in August and September, what you need is a lightweight inconspicuous mac or jacket with a hood which will roll into a convenient bundle to attach to your waist or push into the game-bag outer compartment (this is where I keep mine). One picker up suggested binoculars might be useful for keeping an eye on the progress of the beaters, other pickers up and pricked birds and I can see the point of this suggestion but binoculars, cameras and snacks in the pocket are impediments that I prefer to do without. I am myopic, but after one season's work I got used to the terrain and could see all I needed to with the naked eye.

A picker up on a grouse moor must conceal himself at least 200 yards behind the guns, some shoot captains will ask you to go 300 yards back. The exception is a return drive when you will be told the distance; if you are unsure whether it is a return, ask. I always ask if I am uncertain about this. The picker up must not be visible but ideally should be able to see what is happening, this is usually easy to manage. You conceal yourself and the dogs behind a rock, or a hillock or in a small gulley. Grouse have sharp eyes and excellent hearing and associate the human voice with danger. Bright scarves must be avoided and when all else fades into the background, the distant view of a hatless man remains a white blob visible for miles. Once the drive has started, the pickers up must keep absolutely silent otherwise birds being driven forward which settle in front of the butts will be turned back.

The concept of driving birds on a grouse moor differs fundamentally from pheasant shooting because high birds mean many pricked birds and the moor in general will suffer. The aim of the moor manager is to site his butts so that his grouse come low to them. In October, the grouse will come downwind quite high enough to suit any gun.

The end of the drive will be signalled by a horn blown once to tell the guns to stop shooting in front. By this time the beaters are coming into range and you can usually see them. This is shortly followed by two blasts on the horn to tell the guns to stop shooting and the retrieve can start. Only then, can the picker up move. Collect all dead and wounded grouse which you marked in your patch during the course of the drive and then start to work the dogs in a direct line towards the butts. Young grouse in August

Keepers, loaders and flankers on a Northumberland grouse moor.

frequently come over the butts and drop into the heather behind them, tired but unscathed. Novice pickers up make a beeline for these and of course they lift off and fly away. After several days working on the grouse moor you learn to recognise these young birds and I stop the dogs harassing them until they lift off on their own. Having picked a bird I do like to hold it up to show the gun I believe shot it so that he knows it has been picked, provided he is taking an interest in the pick-up, if he isn't his loader will be. Guns sometimes have their own retrievers and like to use them around their butts. It is bad manners for a picker up to send his dogs hoovering around to assist, he or she should not be there but yards back doing the donkey work picking long fall birds. If there aren't any of these or it is a return drive and you can't go far back, wait until you are asked to help, or until the gun or his loader are finished and have moved away.

Time is of the essence on the grouse moor and there is often pressure to move on to the next drive, but I have never been left behind. It behoves the picker up to work fast but efficiently and to keep an eye on the rest of the party if the next drive is to be on a different part of the moor. I make a point of checking before walking out to my pitch before a drive, where the next drive will be, so that I know how much time we are likely to have for the pick up. Wounded grouse tuck themselves into the heather or under the lip of a burn or peat hag, and can take some finding, especially on a hot day. You must have a retriever which will work without getting wilful. Experience will bring confidence to both dog and handler, marking birds, noting contours, knolls and gulleys and being able to go straight to the fall when the drive is concluded.

Flankers are frequently veterans promoted to the job from the beating line although recently I have seen pickers up occasionally asked to do the job. Flanking may look like an easy option but it is a very important job and needs an experienced person to do it. A flanker will crouch in the heather, three or four on each side of the

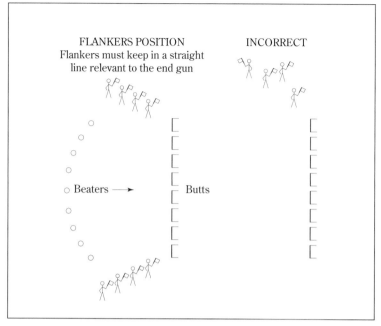

FLANKERS POSITION
Flankers must keep in a straight
line relevant to the end gun

INCORRECT

Beaters →   Butts

Grouse driving.

butts, and pop up waving a flag at crucial moments to turn the birds. The essence of good flanking is surprise, the finesse lies in timing and an inexperienced flanker can ruin a whole drive by showing himself at the wrong moment. The flankers need to be sufficiently close together to ensure that the grouse will not fly in between them after they have been turned by an individual flanker. Grouse flying satisfactorily towards the butts should be left alone, it is infuriating for a keeper to see his birds turned away by over-enthusiastic flankers. I reiterate here that grouse have sharp eyes and flankers must not place themselves on hillocks although they can see better from such a vantage point. Grouse almost always fly around hills and not over them so the flankers sit in the ghylls and valleys and not on the hummocks. On some moors the flankers have a secondary job and have to carry hessian sacks up to the butts to collect the slain birds gathered by the guns' and the loaders' dogs. They then hump them down to the vehicles. I write about flanking here because, unlike the beaters on a grouse moor, flankers may be accompanied by retrievers and can do a useful job after the drive by collecting odd birds they have marked on the edge of the drive. Hence, an experienced picker up may sometimes be asked to help. Should you be fortunate enough to be asked to join the flanking team, you will be told what to do, watch your neighbour carefully and ask for guidelines until you understand the drill. Flanking is essentially teamwork, you work with the others at all times backing each other up.

Chapter 9

Picking Up – Rough Shooting and Beating

Working as a picker up on a rough shooting day is quite different to picking up on a grouse moor or on a driven pheasant or partridge shoot. It can also include acting as a 'stop' at the perimeter of a covert. The term 'rough shooting' covers various forms of the sport but basically implies those shooting outings which do not entail the set party. It is now, usually referred to as 'walked-up' shooting. You cannot say that there are not beaters, implying driven game, because beaters can be very much part of the scene on a rough shoot. Rough shooting also covers solitary hedgerow shooting, dog and man alone or, if the gun is dogless, with a picker up in tow. In a rough shooting scenario, grouse, pheasant, partridge, snipe, woodcock, duck, hare, pigeon and rabbit are all legitimate quarry.

Ideally the rough shooting man's dog will retrieve his game as well as flush it but in practice this seldom works. So the picker up can fill a useful role here by accompanying the walking-up party keeping his or her retriever at heel until needed. For years I worked two dogs, a Spaniel to flush and a Labrador at heel to pick up and it worked very well although I did not have the added responsibility of carrying a gun as well. Better to have two dogs which understand their basic work and execute it correctly than one which is asked to do more than it is capable of and starts to make a nonsense of its work. It takes an exceptional dog and a very competent handler to make a proper job of hunting up the quarry, being rock steady to the flush and then retrieving it on command. The picker up with his, or her responsive, efficient retriever who is working satisfactorily should not be tempted to try the dog in a dual role. I would rather work the hedgerows and brambles and rushy ghylls with our Dachshund than risk my good picking up dogs.

A usual position for a picker up on the rough shoot is with a walking gun, or if the terrain is open pasture and stubble fields, then walking in line with the guns. When I visit the Baker-Cresswells at Preston Tower for their shooting days, some of the work entails standing back from covert as described in previous chapters on driven shooting and also walking with the guns. The dogs walk at heel and I tell them quietly to sit when the line halts or a gun fires. They love it and it is especially useful training for a novice dog. The guns on this type of shoot will stand and walk alternate drives. Sometimes a gun may be asked to walk along the flanks of the beating line to shoot any birds which may erupt from the sides and would probably fly back behind the beating line. The picker up should ask the gun if he would like him to walk with him at the same pace or at a respectful distance behind. I prefer to be behind because I find it easier to mark the birds down but if he wants you to keep pace with him you need to be ready to crouch down should the need arise.

A man or woman acting as a stop will be placed chiefly at the angles of a cover to be beaten or wherever a belt of trees or a hedgerow might enable wily pheasants to run out of the wood unobserved. A stopper should be in position before the sound of guns or the beaters can alert the birds. You need a stick so that you can tap the trunk of a tree with the double object of ensuring your own safety and of preventing the birds from collecting in numbers in the immediate vicinity, because this can lead to an ill-timed flush. The keeper will tell the stop whether he is to fall in with the line of beaters when they come up to him or to remain at their post if it is intended to repeat or reverse the operation on a subsequent drive. There is sometimes opportunity to use your retriever if the line has gone through and a wounded bird is marked down. I very much enjoy acting as a stop on a pheasant shoot because you sometimes stand for half an hour or so, completely alone and silent just inside the covert and I have seen more wildlife doing this job than when I have been picking up. Last season I saw a beautiful orange and white stoat disporting himself on a tree stump in the wintry sun, scratching his ear and rolling on his back. My dogs and I kept quite still and he never saw us and entertained us royally for at least five minutes. We often watch a fox, red squirrel or, occasionally, roe deer.

Should you be asked to beat, it is most likely that you will be able to have your picking up dog at heel although some estates do not tolerate them in the line at all. Those

Beaters on the Ray estate, near Kirkwhelpington in Northumberland.

that are there must be strictly controlled. The average beater is not necessarily a good dog man and, in my experience, beaters' dogs are rarely steady. But beaters are keen and love to work their dogs on a retrieve. Particularly towards the end of the season a picker up may be asked to join the line: I enjoy this, it is getting chilly standing about and I find it rewarding to be with the team and to see the shoot from a different vantage. A responsible beater will watch the effect of any shot that he can see and will mark as nearly as possible the spot where a bird has fallen without breaking the line, should you be near the spot mark it with a stick or a conspicuous stone or leaf in your line of vision. If it is not near enough for your dog to collect without disturbance immediately, then you can go back to it later and follow your mark.

Beating for partridges will mean short drives often over

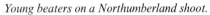

Young beaters on a Northumberland shoot.

pasture or stubble but beaters must be quiet. Partridges seldom fly far but they are scary birds and a covey will swoop into the next field at the sound of a human voice. Partridges are nice birds to retrieve, distances are seldom long and as the birds are small they make a comfortable mouthful for a young dog. Walking through kale, oilseed rape, roots and game crops take a slightly zig-zag line to and fro, because pheasants, especially wily old ones can squat between a line of beaters who easily walk over them. If you are allowed to take a dog in the beating line don't be misled into thinking that you are more important than the next man who only carries a stick. You aren't. However efficient you may become at helping to fill the game bag using your skills as an experienced picker up or beater, you are just a cog in a wheel. Whilst you do contribute to the day's sport you are not indispensable and the shoot can survive without you. The shoot day is organised for the benefit of the guns and not for you or your dog.

Chapter 10

Guidelines – Grouse

In the next two chapters, I have included seven reports from either a shoot manager or head gamekeeper who tell us what they expect from their picking up teams. Living in the North of England myself, I felt it was important to have as wide a brief over Britain as possible because the terrain in which pickers up have to work can vary enormously in different parts of the country. I hope you will find their observations as interesting and helpful as I have. I know that the standard of my picking up work has improved since I read them.

Mark Osborne – (Pennine Sporting) Leaseholder of several top grouse moors

We shoot our moors with a mix of let days, syndicate shooting and my own guest days. Although each of these three types of shooting parties have to some extent different requirements, I believe that the fundamentals relating to picking up are much the same. I confess to being one of those people who believe that the standard of picking up has declined in recent years. I am not exactly sure why this should be, but I suspect it is a combination of fewer dogs belonging to the guns themselves, more commercial shoots with significant numbers of birds shot, and as a consequence, a reliance hitherto not seen on a new type of picker up. In days gone by, the picker up was adjunct to the guns' own dogs and not as is now the case on many shoots, the mainstay of retrieving shot game. On our moors and with the exception of overseas sportsmen, I regard the sight of nine guns, nine Range Rovers and no dogs accompanying the guns as the likely precursor of what will turn out to be an awful day! Sometimes I am proved wrong, but sadly not very often.

My first requirement of a picker up is for he, or she, to actually understand the job they are there to undertake. In my experience few do, and this may be because we shoot owners assume that the pickers up should know what we want without actually telling them. I look at my picking up requirements very simply; I want all the shot grouse picking, but it is the actual guns who are the main players on the field. They are the most important people there (usually because they are paying a great deal of money each day to shoot), and their enjoyment must not be ruined by bad picking up. A gun with a dog must be treated differently from one without. The picker up must appreciate what his or her role is, given differing circumstances appertaining to that particular day.

Unless we are doing a return drive, I like my pickers up to be sitting down out of sight a minimum of 300 yards behind the line of butts. Whilst they and their dogs must not be visible, the picker up should ideally be able to see what is happening. The picker's job during the drive is to mark down hard hit grouse whose landing is often unseen by the guns and then to pick them once the drive is over. At the end of the drive they should stand up and in a direct line work their way in towards the butts. If they pick any grouse they must attract the attention of the gun who they think shot it, and hold it up to show that it has been picked. We find a surprising number of grouse are picked in this way, being far beyond the usual working area of the guns themselves. It is essential that the pickers up clear that ground which is largely out of sight of the guns, picking up those really long fall birds, before moving in to the butts.

If there are very few dogs belonging to guns themselves on a particular day, then it may be necessary to divide the picking up team; some will be charged with picking up as long stops, whilst the remainder will work much closer in.

When the pickers up get close to the butts they should ask if there are any more grouse to pick and if the gun needs a hand. The pickers' dogs should not, at this stage, be hunting as this can be infuriating to the guns trying to reconcile the number of birds picked with those he or she have down. Once the guns have moved on to the next drive a general sweep around the butts should occur. I am much impressed by the approach of the Bollihope keepers when they come to us. One picker up goes to the front of the butts and one to the rear. They position themselves about thirty yards out from the butts themselves and then slowly work all the way down the row of butts, allowing their dogs to hunt widely until they reach the end of the line. This sweeping seems remarkably effective, and finds those grouse which are often mis-marked and are actually much closer in to the butts than the guns think. After a big drive it is amazing how many grouse within fifteen yards of the butts are left unpicked.

My *bête noir* on a grouse moor is the professional dog trainer. I know that there must be exceptions, but the ones I have met are a pain in the neck on a day's grouse shooting. The day is essentially for the guns' enjoyment but it is my hope that everyone else enjoys it as well. It is not, however, the training ground for a dog trainer. If we shoot say, 100 brace over five drives, this means that forty birds have to be picked each drive. Shot grouse are perfectly concealed in heather and on hot, early days take an awful lot of finding. Often the guns may fail to mark accurately their shot birds. It is, therefore, very difficult to be precise during a hectic drive as to where grouse have fallen, so as to be able to tell a picker up where the missing bird is. A picker up with controllable but sweeping dogs is to my mind ideal. A dog which needs to be handled onto a shot bird is of little use on a grouse moor during a day when any serious quantity of grouse are shot.

A keeper with two or three steady, but active dogs is, I think, the best picker up. A field trialer is to be avoided at all costs! When looking over a prominent south of

Scotland moor a few years ago, I was told by the head keeper that 'our pickers up are very professional . . .' My mental picture of a day's shooting on that moor was not complimentary! I would much rather have one or two enthusiastic amateurs who keep on looking for the missing grouse. All too often I see pickers up walk away from where they have been told a grouse is missing, apparently believing that if their dogs cannot find it, then it cannot be there. Perseverance is often a much better attribute in both a dog and its handler than breeding, certificates of merit or even field trial championships.

Finally I would comment on the attitude of pickers up on the shooting field. I want a happy environment where the guns are being assisted by a willing, cheerful and enthusiastic team. Too often the pickers up seem to resent either the guns, the terrain, the lack of, or on occasions I have even seen, the presence of too many grouse. Good pickers up are both vital and a real asset to a day's shooting. Bad ones frequently mar a day.

Kenny Wilson – Head Keeper on Leadhill Moor for twenty-eight years. Now the Grouse Adviser for the Game Conservancy and Grouse Consultant for Savills

Grouse shooting, whether walked up or driven shooting, should never be attempted without men with good dogs. Hiring of pickers up should be undertaken by the head keeper, and a good man will see to it that he hires keen dog handlers, whether they be amateur or professional. On driven days, three pickers up with at least two dogs each are ideal.

Before shooting begins, the head keeper may appoint one man in charge of the others and will take that man to every drive and show him where the pickers up should be placed. Unless there is going to be a return drive, the pickers up should be behind the guns, out of shot range but where they can see around them. They should be looking for wounded grouse within the area that they are responsible for at the back and not any birds falling around the guns. Three pickers up can cover a line of eight or nine guns and they should look for, and mark down within this area, all obviously wounded grouse, birds which tower, birds which suddenly leave the covey and birds which, when passing by, have an audible breathing difficulty. Dead or wounded birds may have fallen quite some distance from the handler and a good, well-trained dog which can be handled on to a given spot will save a lot of time. These grouse should be looked for and collected first.

When the long birds are all picked, the handlers should then begin to move towards the butts. If the guns are still there, they should then ask what birds may have been shot and the area where they may be lying. Once the guns have moved on, the handlers or pickers up should then line up behind the butts hoovering an area of about fifty yards parallel with the butts from one end of the line to the other. This will entail all of the dogs hunting their area as they move forward. The same procedure should be carried out at the front of the butt line, back to the beginning. This procedure is very important to ensure a very clean pick up. If there is a return drive, the pickers up should stand at either end of the gun line where they can see behind and mark down long birds. These grouse can be retrieved when the return drive is over.

The calibre of the dog handler is very important and a good head keeper will look for good men whether they be amateur or professional. A good amateur handler must be keen and willing to try for the most doubtful of wounded birds but few can handle their dogs out to a distant spot. They have to go there with the dogs. There are a lot of good professional handlers but they also must be keen. All of them will appear with many dogs, up to about eight in number, all of the dogs will be very steady, but the younger dogs may not work very much and they will be there for experience. The professional handler will be able to send dogs out a great distance which is an advantage and the men themselves are mostly very pleasant especially to the guns as they may be looking to sell a dog or two.

Here are few words of warning from my experience:

Beware of the picker up who appears around the butts almost as soon as the drive is over.

Beware of the one who spends a lot of time talking to the guns or wanting to sit at a butt.

Beware of the one who is reluctant to go after a bird which has dropped a long way off.

Beware of one who has dogs out of control, which chase other dogs or are constantly looking for a fight or which chase hare into the next parish, or spend half the day with their head down a rabbit hole.

A good head keeper will always ensure that he finds the right quality of man and dogs for the job.

Chapter 11

Guidelines –
Pheasant and Partridge

Hugh Cheswright – Shoot Organiser, Wallington,
Northumberland

Over the years I have come to the conclusion that a good picking up team will add anything from five to ten per cent to the bag and in Northumberland we are fortunate to have so many people who are willing to work their dogs for the sheer joy of it. However there is a world of difference between having a willing and enthusiastic picker up and one who really understands the craft and the etiquette which is involved. There is nothing more irritating than a merry band of pickers up working their dogs, 100 yards behind a line of guns, picking up everything in range whilst totally ignoring the pricked birds that fly on and pitch into another wood and out of sight. Overcoming this problem has to be the responsibility of the shoot organiser. The guns, pickers up and beaters should know exactly what is expected of them at each stage of a day's shooting.

I always discuss the detail of each day's shooting with the keepers prior to the event. We cover the proposed drives, the number of stops required and where the pickers up will need to stand. On the morning of the shoot I confirm the agreed plan or modify it, depending on the weather conditions, and advise the pickers up and beaters accordingly. Where possible I keep the pickers up with the guns, as they are usually easier to place once the guns are in position. This has the added advantage of making the guns aware of the location of each picker up and makes it easier for the guns to advise on where they think their birds have fallen.

The pickers up have strict instructions to concentrate on the pricked and wounded birds which fall at least 300 yards from the shooting line and not to come forward until they have picked these birds. Under no circumstances are they permitted to pick any birds close to a gun without the gun's approval, and in particular, any gun who is working a dog. After all, many shooters get immense pleasure from working their dogs, and it is very vexing when you have a picker up do the job unasked.

As there are usually one or two hard runners at each drive, I always leave one picker up behind at each drive to mop up. They are told where the next drive will be and where they should stand, and usually catch up before the drive actually starts.

My pickers up get paid the same rate as the beaters, and the whole team gets a brace of pheasants as a bonus at least twice during the season, plus a keepers' day shoot at the end of January.

As with most activities which involve a number of people, the criteria is to get the planning right. If guns, keepers, pickers up and beaters are clear about what is expected of them, everyone can have a happy and enjoyable day. Sometimes even the shoot organiser can have an enjoyable day too, when things go according to plan.

W. G. Meldrum – Head Keeper, Norfolk

On this estate we have a simple system of picking up which has been used for a number of years. We have our pickers up on our shoots who stay well back (around 300 yards) in the open ground. All will be in position on the first drive. For the second drive two of the pickers up move on with the guns and the other two stay behind and pick up from the first drive. The first drive pickers then get in position for the third drive, leaving the second drive pickers to clear up after the guns and pick up any remaining birds. The system continues in this way for all the drives. As our drives are somewhat close together all four pickers up may end up together for some of the drives. It is a pleasure to see a good team of pickers up working closely together thus ensuring a clean and tidy shoot.

Although there are some good field trial dogs, we tend to use straight forward pickers up. They seem not to hang about around the guns for dog training, but concentrate solely on picking up.

Michael Halford – Captain of the Hamerton Shoot, Cambridgeshire

I write this from the perspective of a gun, and the organiser of the Hamerton Shoot, where main shooting is south of the Humber and east of the M1. Can I identify anything that makes the needs of a shoot here any different from one, for example, in the north – are the guns better or worse? More polite, perhaps? Whose dogs run in? Is there a language barrier? The fact is, that any participant can join in a shooting party anywhere around the country and feel at home with what goes on. There is such a wide diversity of skills in all departments. The difference, if there is one, must lie in the climate and the geography.

The 'south' encompasses the wide open spaces of the eastern counties as well, with fewer woods and a lack of meaningful hills, alongside the heavily wooded home counties and on to the 1,000-foot downs with their sheer-sided valleys and hanging woods. In the mainly arable fields of many of our eastern counties these are large, and woodland can be in short supply. Frequent use is made of sugar beet and other root crops, as well as specially-sited patches of field cover. Maize, canary grass, kale and quinoa are all there, as well as other species which could be weeds but turn out to be hiding infant tree plantations.

Many drives make use of these outside coverts, along with the pheasants' natural homing instinct, to provide the incentive and opportunity for the birds to achieve a testing altitude and velocity.

Partridges, wild fen pheasants and even reared pheasants from coverts which we have on our shoot will fly considerable distances, so the team of pickers up must be prepared to stand well back from the action, sometimes several hundred yards back and missing all the fun! Tales of who shot well, who missed what and whose dog ran in will all have to wait. The area immediately behind the line should present few problems and can be swept up later, although birds lying in furrows can be surprisingly hard to find.

In these circumstances, the team need to know their ground. They must mark like hawks, even to the extent of having a forward observer calling back, and using binoculars. It is vital that pickers up are well briefed and that they are quite clear where they can and cannot go. They need to have a vehicle to be able to follow on in their own time. There is nothing more embarrassing for the field master than finding that he has left a gun behind somewhere. But losing, or worse still, forgetting, a picker up is a pretty heinous offence as well.

On our shoot the pickers up are regulars. They know the ground and where the wounded birds are likely to end up. We have a team of ladies and I suspect that they provide a civilising influence on our guns and are certainly not overawed by them. They are quick to spot the gun whose claims cannot always be relied on and they know whose birds will be found stone dead behind the lines (frequently young men who are deadly with their twenty-bores). The pickers up join the guns for lunch and our day is immeasurably better and brighter for their presence.

What do I not want in a picker up? I hate professional handlers using their dogs as hoovers, working close behind me. I find it off-putting, to say the least, and to have stray dogs working around me and picking up birds in the middle of the drive makes it very hard to keep count and to mark. My own dog may not be the best in the world, but when I take him out shooting I do want him to have a chance of looking for my birds first, and to enjoy his day. It greatly enhances mine.

I do not like the 'been there, done that' picker up who appears out of a covert, claims to have cleared it and brushes off any attempts to help. They may be right, but often seem to ignore efforts to describe a damaged bird that has flown on.

Mocking cries from the beating line at the inadequacies of my guns may not be welcome but are, nevertheless, understandable after a trudge through fire and flood for nothing. But from the pickers up I need sympathy and understanding that the guns cannot always be deadly.

That leaves me with a small list of desirable attributes for my pickers up: close attention to the briefing and careful planning; meticulous marking and persistent searching, with excellent dog control giving one hundred per cent success rate. Is this too much to ask? Probably, but at least we have a target.

Roger Foster – Head Keeper, Swinburne Estate, Northumberland

After six months of work on the rearing field and trying to keep birds in the coverts – at last the shooting season is about to start. What the gamekeeper needs to do before his covert days begin, is to plan his teams of beaters and pickers up. The other team on the day will be the guns. The three groups should work smoothly together and the day will, hopefully, be enjoyed by them all.

For a team of eight guns I like to have three pickers up. Some of the guns will have their own dogs, so the pickers up should stand well back marking birds that the guns may not even be aware that they have hit. The guns with dogs often like to pick up their own birds, so they should

Roger Foster (right) talks to one of his team.

be given time and space to do this. The pickers up should work their way in and clean up in the area nearest the guns and may be given the 'fall' details of a bird that has not yet been picked.

The guns will move on to the next drive and the pickers up will still be sweeping the ground for the last few birds. They should have been told the order of the drives and a good team often turns up behind the guns just a few minutes before the first birds come over the pegs.

For a single-handed keeper, a good team of pickers up can take a great deal of pressure off him on shooting days. They often drive the game cart, brace and hang the shot game, even hanging the birds in the game larder at the end of the day.

What makes a good picker up? Two or three good,

On some pheasant shoots a picker up may be experienced to drive or to load up the game cart.

David Hitchings, Gurston Down, who gives his guidelines.

steady dogs which can sweep a big area or stick to a runner. Good eyesight! It is amazing how often guns are not aware of having hit a bird, especially in the heat of a big flush. And finally, sticking power. They will have to make sure that every last bird has been picked, and not want to be off to the next drive in a hurry.

78

David Hitchings – Head Keeper of Gurston Down Shoot in Wiltshire for over thirty years

Gurston Down Shoot has always been very popular with pickers up because of the open nature of the terrain behind the guns. Field trialists especially appreciate this because they like to direct their dogs over long distances with whistle and hand signals. It is also very popular with shoot pickers up because they enjoy watching the shooting in the distance, especially if a known good shot is in the party, to see how he handles the challenge of high pheasants and partridges; most of which in fact are very seldom out of shot.

When my keeper, Eric Penny, selects his pickers up for a new season he has a number of strict priorities. Firstly, all dogs must be very steady and under full control at all times. He tends to prefer the larger dogs as they are often a little bit quieter but one cannot get away from the fact that really well controlled Spaniels can be excellent. Secondly, a new picker up is told that he, or she, is not allowed anywhere near a release pen because at certain times of the day they could be full of tired pheasants. I still wince when I think of a new picker many years ago who was found outside the gates of one of the release pens with a large number of birds all neatly braced up and obviously very few had been shot. Eric would also ask that they be very sensitive to the gun who wants to use his own dog sometimes on birds that are quite a long way back. We encourage our pickers up to be very courteous but firm, with the optimistic gun who, on almost every drive, has a bird which wobbled a bit and must be looked for regardless of how far it may have gone. In this situation, the picker up has a number of stock answers such as, 'Sorry sir, we are not allowed back there because that is a drive we are doing later today . . .' I do remember one new picker up here at Gurston Down who went up to a gun and said 'Our job would be a lot easier if you shot the birds where the corn goes in and not where it comes out.' Ouch! This picker up did not come again.

Most of our pickers up stand 200 yards behind the line of guns. Should a bird which has quite obviously been wounded land near them, and there is a danger of it running off, then it should be picked up immediately, even if the drive is still in progress. After a drive is over it is always a good sight to see four or five pickers up sweeping the ground right up to the gun line to collect that one bird that can so often be missed near the pegs.

Appendix 1

Gundog Trainers who offer individual, or group training for pickers up

Edward Martin
Sealpin Kennels
Lanton Hill Farm
Jedburgh, Roxburghshire
TD8 6SY

Tel: 01835 863275

First-class kennels and training facilities with a rabbit pen.

Walter Harrison
Sunstar Gundog Training Centre
Beacon Hill Cottage
West Morden
Nr Wareham, Dorset
BH20 7EA

Tel: 01929 459364

Courses specifically arranged to suit both new and experienced pickers up. Mixed courses and some 'ladies' only. Good training facilities.

Guy Wallace
Warren Gundogs
Llandefalle, Brecon
LD3 0ND

Tel: 01874 754311

George Ridley
Shadowbrae Gundogs
East Deanraw

Langley-on-Tyne, Northumberland
NE47 5LY

Tel: 01434 684683

Private tuition. Courses arranged to suit novice and experienced handlers.

Christopher McHugh
The Ewen Gundog Training Centre
Bittenam Springs
Ewen
Cirencester, Glos.
GL7 6BY

Tel: 01285 770474
Fax: 01285 770169

Private lessons or group tuition. Residential courses for pickers up arranged to suit client.

Mrs Joanne Walters
Bearley Farm
Tintinhull
Yeovil, Somerset
BA22 8PE

Tel: 01935 822033

Gundog training weekends.

Mrs Gay Hanbury
East Farmhouse
Piddlehinton
Dorchester, Dorset
ET2 7TD

Tel: 01300 348465

Dorset shoot days for young dogs and potential pickers up (Game Conservancy)

CONTRAIL GUNDOGS
Frances Brooks
Mossend
Corsock
Castle Douglas
DG7 3ED

Tel: 01644 440229

Good facilities and thorough training for pickers up as well as guns accompanied by dogs. Trainees stay in the Urr Valley Hotel and Frances' husband, Chris, dishes up first-class lunches at Mossend. All the dogs and handlers improved immensely on the intermediate course which I attended. Highly recommended.

Appendix 2

Humane Gamebird Dispatchers

William Powell and Son
35 Carrs Lane
Birmingham
B4 7SX

Tel: 01216 438362

W. A. M. (R. J. Payne)
Warren Farm Cottage
Headly Lane
Mickleham
Dorking, Surrey
RH5 6DG

Tel: 01372 377279

Appendix 3

Further Reading

The Shooting Man's Dog (A Complete Guide to Gundogs)
David Hudson, Swan Hill Press, £19.95

Includes a comprehensive few pages on picking up

Gundog Sense and Sensibility
Wilson Stephens, Pelham Books, £9.95

Full of commonsense advice and some worthwhile comments on picking up work

Gundog Training
Keith Erlandson, Swan Hill Press, £16.95

Includes a useful chapter on picking up

A Dog at Heel
Veronica Heath, Boydell and Brewer, £9.95

Several chapters on picking up. Scarce. Currently reprinting, McCarthy and Bassett, publishers

Gundogs – Their Learning Chain
Joe Irving, Swan Hill Press, £14.95

A chapter on picking up and beating. Useful reading and I liked his comments on game sense

Retriever Training
Susan Scales, Swan Hill Press, £15.95

Short useful comment on picking up

Getting It Right with Gundogs
Graham Cox and Martin Deeley, published by the Game Conservancy 1985

Advanced Gundog Training
Martin Deeley, Crowood Press, £14.95

Includes a chapter on picking up

The Complete Gundog
John Humphreys, David and Charles, £17.95

Chapter on picking up and on rough shooting, both helpful

The above books are helpful for pickers up. If you cannot find them in book shops or in a library, the Kennel Club in Clarges Street, Piccadilly, have all of them and allowed me to browse. There are plenty more, but I found the above titles especially helpful.

Appendix 4

Useful Addresses

The Kennel Club
1–5 Clarges Street
London W1Y 8AB

Tel: 0171 493 6651

British Association for Shooting and Conservation
Marford Mill, Chester Road
Rossett, Wrexham
Clwyd LL12 0HL

Tel: 01244 573000
Fax: 01244 573001

British Field Sports Society and Countryside Alliance
367 Kennington Road
London SE11 4PT

Tel: 0171 582 5432
Fax: 0171 793 8484

Game Conservancy Trust
Fordingbridge
Hampshire
SP6 1EF

Tel: 01425 652381
Fax: 01425 655848

Appendix 5

Do's and Dont's

1 Do remember that the shoot day is primarily arranged for the enjoyment of the guns present.

2 Do remember that the shoot organiser and/or the head keeper are the men to look up to. Their orders must be complied with at all times.

3 Do remember that the ambience of the day is very important and a happy, compatible team will contribute to this.

4 Do keep an eye on your transport.

5 Do not speak ill of someone's else's dog.

6 Do not shout.

7 Do not repeat gossip.

Index